HEREWARD

Outlaw and Hero

IN MEMORIAM
PETER REX
1930 - 2012

PETER REX
WRITTEN FOR AND PUBLISHED BY THE ELY SOCIETY

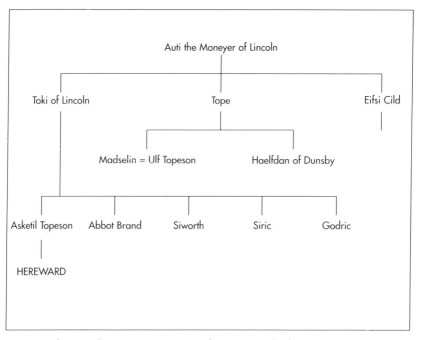

Hereward's Family Descent. Copyright Peter and Christina Rex.

HEREWARD

Outlaw and Hero

Hereward, the famous outlaw, was the nephew of Abbot Brand of Peterborough and his father was one of the Abbot's brothers, called Asketil. Abbot Brand had in fact four brothers: Asketil, the eldest, a King's Thegn, and three younger brothers, Siward, Siric and Godric. The three younger brothers were all still alive after 1086 and were too young for any one of them to have been Hereward's father. The five brothers were all sons of a rich merchant, called Toki, of Lincoln.

Asketil the King's Thegn was a rich nobleman with land in at least five counties and the Domesday Book shows that he was also known as Asketil of Ware. A King's Thegn (the word is pronounced 'thane') was one of the nobles who served King Edward the Confessor, carrying out his orders and seeing to it that others obeyed the king. If there had been no Norman Conquest, Hereward would have become a King's Thegn in his turn, after his father's death.

In the year 1063, Abbot Osketil of Crowland had begun the building of a new Abbey Church, and for this he needed to raise plenty of money. One way of doing so was to rent out the Abbey lands to local lords who would pay an annual sum to the monastery, and one of those who agreed to do so was a young man of eighteen called Hereward Asketilson. He was the son of a wealthy local Thegn in the service of King Edward the Confessor, and the Abbot thought this man would be reliable. He was wrong. Hereward had agreed to rent a farm at Rippingale near Bourne in Lincolnshire for a sum of money to be agreed with the Abbot at the beginning of each year and, at the end of the first year, Hereward and the Abbot quarrelled over the rent. The Abbot complained to his father who mentioned the matter to the King. Hereward had already upset many people in the towns and villages of South Lincolnshire, causing disturbances and generally making trouble for everyone.

The King was furious and said he would give Hereward five days in which to leave the Kingdom or it would be the worse for him. Hearing this, Hereward did not wait around and fled. Some said that he went to Northumbria, as far from Winchester (then the capital city) as he could get and still be in England, where he met an escaped performing bear and killed it. Others claimed that he fled to Ireland, to the King of Dublin and Leinster, whose name was Dermot, and fought in his wars. While there, he was said to have helped the King's son to carry off a noble lady, daughter of a former King of Cornwall, so that he could marry her.

The truth is that, like other exiled Englishmen at that time, he took ship for Flanders and, as it was by now autumn, the season of storms in the Channel, he was shipwrecked on the coast of Guines and taken prisoner. Guines, which lay between Boulogne and Calais, was then ruled by Count Manasses the Old, who was in charge of dealing with all men shipwrecked on that coast. Having told the Count who he was and that he was of noble birth, Hereward was released. In order to earn a living, he began a career as a mercenary soldier, at first in the service of Wulfric Rabel, who commanded the castle of St. Omer. While there, he quarrelled with a Breton knight called Hoibricht, fought a duel with him, and won. As a result of this victory, a noble lady of St. Omer, Turfrida by name, fell in love with him.

At this time, in France and Flanders, a new sport among fighting men was just becoming popular, an early form of Tournament in which groups of men, sometimes on foot and sometimes on horseback, fought each other watched by a large crowd. Hereward naturally couldn't resist taking part and he fought at Poitiers in France and Bruges in Flanders, winning a reputation as a tough and skilled competitor. On one of these occasions he met the lady Turfrida, who already fancied him, fell in love and married her.

Hearing that Lietbert, Bishop and Count of Cambrai, was in need of soldiers, Hereward joined his army and became one of the twelve knights who were his bodyguards. The Bishop was busy defending his lordship over Cambrai against John and Hugh of Arras who commanded the castle there, and Hereward was very useful to the Bishop. He also took part in other small wars in the area between such lords as Baldwin II of Hainault, a grandson of the Count of Flanders, and Arnulf the Viscount of Picquigny. (Flanders and Hainault are now part of southern Belgium.) Hereward was noticed by Baldwin II's uncle, Robert the Frisian. (Frisia was the original coast of Holland before land was reclaimed from the sea.) Robert was planning a campaign on behalf of his father, Count Baldwin V, who had decided to recapture the area then called Scaldemariland, that is, the islands at the mouth of the River Scheldt.

The idea was to force the people of these islands, especially that of Walcheren, to pay money to the Count as they used to do to his grandfather. They were then refusing to pay. So Robert the Frisian set out in forty ships with an army under his personal command and took Hereward with him as commander of the mercenary soldiers. Hereward also had to train the younger, newly knighted men. Fierce fighting followed the attack and at first the islanders resisted so stubbornly that Robert had to fall back and call for reinforcements. The islanders boasted later that they had captured their enemy's battle flag, which was considered a great achievement. The battle flag, or standard, was carried into battle. Soldiers would rally round the flag during the battle and it was a great disgrace to lose it. Modern army regiments still have such standards, calling them 'the Colours'.

The Count's son then launched a stronger attack against the islands because the whole area had risen up against him. He was attacked from all sides, from the islands and from the sea. The invaders landed on the island of Walcheren, attacking its defences, and Hereward, in what became his trademark in war, suggested setting fire to the enemy wagons. He led a force of 300 men ahead of the main army and they killed many hundreds of men. He followed that up by taking the high ground with a force of 1,000 knights and 600 footsoldiers and then attacked the enemy in the rear, killing the rearguard. That was too much for the islanders who asked for peace in order to discuss the renewal of their former treaty with the Count who insisted on the money due being doubled. Hereward said that he and his men would keep all the plunder they had seized during the fighting. With part of his share, Hereward bought himself two fine horses for his own use, calling his favourite one "Swallow".

Just as this success was being celebrated, Count Baldwin V died and was succeeded by his elder son, also called Baldwin, much to the annoyance of Robert the Frisian who was the younger brother. That meant an end to Robert's campaign in Scaldemariland and of Hereward's work as a soldier, but he had become quite rich as a result of his various campaigns.

At this time, Hereward heard that England had been conquered by the Normans and, leaving his wife Turfrida in the care of two of his cousins, Siward the Red and Siward the Blond, he decided to return to England and find out what had happened to his family. Once there, he found that his father Asketil and his grandfather Toki, a rich merchant of Lincoln, had died in the fighting as well as his younger brother, Toli, so he decided to join those Englishmen known by the Normans as 'Wildmen of the Woods', who were fighting against the Normans. Although the English had at first been ready to accept King William's rule, they had become more and more angry about the way the Norman barons and knights were behaving. There had been widespread looting and the lands of those who had died in the three battles of 1066 had been given to Norman barons. Those left in charge of the kingdom when King William returned to Normandy to celebrate his victory had done nothing to control their men.

The rebels had taken refuge in woods, marshes and river valleys and Hereward, who had been born in South Lincolnshire, now returned to the area he knew best, the Fens. He first visited his uncle, Brand the Monk, who had succeeded Abbot Leofric as Abbot of Peterborough. Abbot Leofric had returned sick at heart from the Battle of Hastings, and died of his wounds. Brand had angered King William by going to the English Prince, Edgar, for recognition as Abbot because William had not, at that time, been crowned king. King William had made him pay a fine of 40 marks of gold because the Abbot had not recognised that he, William, was King of England. This was a huge sum of money for those days, perhaps ten thousand pounds in today's money.

Hereward had held some of his lands as protector of Peterborough, and now renewed his promise to protect the abbey. But he also found that all his lands and those of his father and grandfather, in more than seven shires, had been taken by the Normans. Hereward's own lands went to a Breton knight called Ogier. Several great Norman lords had shared out his family lands, men such as Bishop Remigius of Dorchester, who had moved his Bishop's Seat to Lincoln and was building Lincoln Cathedral on land once held by Hereward's grandfather, Toki. Others who had got rich in this way included Ivo Taillebois, Sheriff of Lincolnshire, William de Warenne, later Earl of Surrey, and a Flanders knight, brother-in-law of Warenne, named Frederick Oosterzele-Scheldewindeke. As a start to his campaign against the Normans, Hereward waylaid Frederick and killed him.

Basing himself in a hideout in the Fens, and given help by the Abbot of Ely, named Thurstan, Hereward began harassing the Normans, killing and robbing them, so that King William himself was forced to offer him a truce after he almost caught and killed William de Warenne. Hereward then decided to return to Flanders to collect his wife Turfrida and bring her to England, and also to recruit some of those who had served with him in Scaldemariland. While there he received messages from Abbot Thurstan telling him his uncle, Brand, was dead and that the sons of Swein Estrithson, King of Denmark, had arrived in the Fens with a raiding army and might be persuaded to support a rising against the Normans. He was also told that King William had appointed a Norman as abbot of Peterborough, Turold of Malmesbury, who was on his way to the abbey with an army of Normans. King William was said to have chosen him because he was a warlike and quarrelsome man and that as he liked fighting, he, William, would give him someone to fight with, meaning Hereward.

Hereward got his men together and returned hurriedly to England. He held a meeting with the Danes and talked them into helping him upset King William's plan by seizing all the wealth and treasures of Peterborough to prevent them from falling into Norman hands. Gathering his combined force of Englishmen, Danes and former mercenaries,

Hereward advanced to the attack on Peterborough, crossing the Fens in large flat-bottomed boats, by way of the Wellstream near Outwell, seeking to gain entry by way of the Bolhythe Gate south of the Abbey. At first unable to gain entry and resisted by the townsfolk, Hereward and his men set fire to the gate and to all the town buildings outside the walls of the monastery, so causing a great deal of confusion and giving the monks ample time to get out before his men and the Danes broke in.

Once inside, they set about collecting everything movable of value they could lay their hands on. They tried to remove the Great Crucifix, laden with gold and precious stones, hanging at the entry to the High Altar but could only take the crown from the head of the figure of Christ and the golden footrest at its feet. But elsewhere they were more successful, taking eleven decorated boxes (in which were carried the relics of saints), encrusted with gold, silver and precious stones, twelve jewelled crosses and many other objects of gold and silver, books with jewelled covers, and the huge altar hanging, also embroidered in precious metals and jewels.

Leaving the area around the monastery devastated by the fire and the abbey stripped of most of its most precious possessions, especially the arm of St. Oswald, the raiders retreated, hearing that Abbot Turold and his men had reached Stamford in Lincolnshire and were on their way to Peterborough. With them of their own accord went Prior Aethelwold and several senior monks. Only one lonely monk was left behind, Leofwine the Tall, who was lying ill in the Infirmary. Despite the fire, no serious damage was done and Turold was able to resume church services within a week of his arrival. No monks had been harmed, either.

Then, from Hereward's point of view, everything started to go pear-shaped. The Danes hung on to the greater portion of the booty and refused to assist in further resistance to the Normans. Instead, they were ordered by King Swein, who had done a deal with King William in return for a large bribe, to return to Denmark, so leaving Hereward and his men to face King William's wrath. The Danes had little profit out of the attack, though. On their journey home they ran into a storm and most of their ships were wrecked with the loss of men and treasure. Some did make it back to Denmark only to lose more when the church they took over caught fire. Prior Aethelwold and his monks were allowed to return to England and managed to save St. Oswald's arm, and most of the other relics.

Hereward and his men now took refuge at Ely and held out for several months against all the efforts of local Norman lords, such as Ivo Taillebois, aided by Abbot Turold, to dislodge them. Hereward's force continued to harry the Normans at every opportunity, even, on one

Ely from Stuntney. The Great Ouse in Flood. R. Farren 1883

occasion, surrounding Abbot Turold and a company of men, only releasing them on payment of a ransom of some hundreds of pounds, equal to hundreds of thousands in today's money.

Hereward at Ely became a magnet for rebel Englishmen, some, like himself, of Danish descent, who joined him there. If he agreed to let them join him, he made them swear to stick together against the Normans. They had to make their promise over the tomb of St. Etheldreda. Many of his supporters were his relatives from Lincolnshire and he was joined by another Dane, called Thorkell of Harringworth, who had lost his lands in Northamptonshire. Yet another supporter was the rich landowner Siward of Maldon in Essex. Rahere, called the Heron, from Wroxham on the Bure in the Broads, Brother Siward from the Abbey of Bury St. Edmunds, Reginald, who was Hereward's Standard Bearer, and many, many more, all joined the cause.

These men carried out pillaging raids against the Normans far and wide, sometimes suffering heavy losses themselves, and their warfare reassured many people that all was not yet lost. For a time, King William himself did nothing, leaving the task of dealing with Hereward to local barons such as William de Warenne from Castle Acre, William Malet from Eye in Suffolk and Richard fitzGilbert from Clare. But following the rising of 1069 when the whole of Northern England, led by Prince Edgar, the last Saxon heir to the throne, and Earl Waltheof, rebelled against King William, only to be defeated at York, something happened to change the King's mind.

Two of the last surviving Earls from King Edward's time, the brothers Edwin, Earl of Mercia and Morcar, Earl of Northumbria, had at last lost all faith in King William. Edwin had been promised a daughter of the King as his wife, but nothing came of it, and the Earls feared that, as part of his revenge for the rising, which had caused William to burn and destroy Yorkshire and Durham in the "Harrying of the North", they too would be imprisoned. They therefore escaped from their "house arrest" at the King's court and for six months hid out in woods and fields, evading capture.

At last, hoping to find a ship and escape to Flanders, they arrived at Ely, accompanied by a few other nobles and their household troops. One companion was the great landowner Siward Barn, another was Ordgar, Sheriff of Cambridgeshire, also Bishop Aethelwine of Durham. There were also two more of Edwin and Morcar's relatives, Godric of Corby and Tostig of Daventry. They had all met up at Welle in the Fens, near Wisbech, and persuaded Hereward to allow them to spend the winter with his rebels at Ely. These were men who had come south, seeking to flee to the continent, unlike Prince Edgar and Maerleswein, the English sheriff of Lincolnshire and their supporters, who had sought refuge in Scotland.

So now the last shreds of opposition to King William were all gathered together in one place and William could not resist the opportunity. But to deal with them was not going to be easy. Ely was an island surrounded by Fens and almost impregnable. The rivers, the deep, almost bottomless meres, and the marshes surrounding the Isle made it a tremendous obstacle to any army, especially one like the Norman army, whose strength lay in cavalry. Any attempt at a waterborne assault could be easily repelled. The available ways onto the Isle from Earith, Soham or Downham-in-the-Isle, were well known, difficult and could be guarded. The defenders had built ramparts of peat surmounted by strong fences from which javelins and missiles of all kinds could be launched. King William also realised that a large fighting force in such an easily defended position, well stocked with food and water, could hold out almost indefinitely, and, commanded as it was by Hereward, a soldier of proven ability, it was not going to be a walkover.

The Chronicles of the time record King William's moves. He called out naval and land forces on a large scale, setting his ships to blockade the Isle from the seaward (or northern) side, and surrounding the rest of the Isle on the landward side. All accounts of the King's attack are confused, but what took place is clear enough. King William gathered his best soldiers and his commanders together at the castle in Cambridge and planned an attack which first meant crossing the fen at its narrowest point by strengthening an existing causeway. This was a very old track called the Mare's Way, running from Willingham to a former Iron Age earthwork called Belsar's Hill. Having got there, he quickly set up camp, building a new palisade or fence along the top of the rampart of the earthwork. He then ordered all the local English to provide him with materials with which he could continue to build his causeway and make some sort of bridge by which he could cross the Old West River onto the Isle. (In Old English, the word for "bridge" and that for "causeway" are the same, which has given rise to a great deal of confusion ever since.)

While King William was busy, so was Hereward, carrying out scouting forays, building up stocks of food and weapons, and killing or wounding any parties of Normans found away from their base.

The Conqueror's Route to Aldreth

King William had set up an advance post at Devil's Dyke, near Reach, and some men from there attempted to cross the West River below where it was joined by the River Cam. They used heaps of wood and bags of sand and tried to make the swirling bed of the river fordable. However, Hereward had seen this as a weak spot and fortified the area with walls of peat and the Normans were easily repulsed. Hereward then counter-attacked at Reach. A small party of seven men led by Hereward himself attacked the outpost and killed all the men guarding it except one, called Richard, son of Osbert, saying it was not fitting for seven men to attack the one man left standing. It was a sound move because Richard later told the King's Council of War what had happened and how Hereward had gone on to burn down the nearby village of Burwell before retreating as reinforcements were brought up.

Meanwhile, King William had moved to a point on the West River not far from the modern hamlet of Aldreth, but some way to the east, where the fen was narrower than elsewhere. There he set about rather hurriedly building a floating structure loosely called a bridge, supported, according to one account, by sheepskins filled with air. A more credible version of that says they were full of sand. It is possible that the local peasant labourers used to build it sabotaged the structure. It was certainly not well designed.

As soon as it seemed to be ready, and before the defenders could react, a large number of Norman knights and men-at-arms rushed onto the bridge, eager to be first on the Isle with its promise of rich plunder. That was a disaster! The whole thing was so unstable that it collapsed, throwing all the men on it into the river and the surrounding swamp so that they were all, save one, swallowed up in the water. One man made it across before the collapse, a knight called Deda, who was immediately captured by the defenders and taken before Hereward.

King William, appalled at the loss of life, some hundreds at least had perished, retreated in despair to the former royal manor of Brampton, near Huntingdon, to lick his wounds. Meanwhile, Hereward was entertaining Deda the knight, making sure he saw exactly what Hereward wanted him to see and no more. Deda was well looked after and invited to dine in the refectory of Ely monastery along with Abbot Thurstan and his monks and the various noble supporters of Hereward. They feasted at great wooden trestle tables in the hall with their arms and armour stacked against the walls ready for use and their shields hanging on the walls behind their seats. Deda was carefully allowed to think that the defenders were well supplied with food from the abbey lands and water from its wells, and that they could harvest more from the woods and meres of the Fens, as well as the famous eels of Ely, and wine from its vineyard. He was then set free so that he could report all this to King William.

At a meeting of the King's council, Deda did exactly that, and almost persuaded the King to give up his attack on Ely. But Ivo Taillebois, in a dramatic speech, persuaded the king that he would never live down such a defeat. He also argued that he knew of a famous Fenland witch, called a Pythoness because she foretold the future by means of a great snake. He said that she could be prevailed upon to curse the Islanders so that their nerve failed and they could then be defeated. These arguments persuaded the King to try again and work began on a new portable bridge guarded by two tall wooden siege towers. These were huge platforms on wheels which could be used to fire missiles at the opposite bank of the river to drive back the defenders, and the witch could stand on top of one of them to work her spells and curse them.

However, Hereward had not left Deda to return alone, but had followed him and so located the King's camp at Brampton. There he hid his horse Swallow, disguised himself as a seller of pots and oil lamps and infiltrated the Norman camp. Once there, he listened in carefully to what was being said about the King's plans and heard all about the new bridge with its siege towers and the plan to employ a witch to curse the islanders. He discovered where she was and was able to spy on her when she went into the swamp to consult her guardian spirit (perhaps it was a giant eel) and begin her spells. Hereward determined that she would soon be dealt with.

On his return to the camp he was seen by one of the King's men who said that this so-called seller of pots was really Hereward the notorious outlaw. Hereward strongly denied the accusation, claiming to hate Hereward 'that man of Belial', against whom he claimed to want his own revenge. But once the trouble started, a crowd gathered and began to taunt Hereward, picking on him as a stupid fellow, breaking his pots, pulling his beard and trying to cut off all his hair. He was pushed and shoved and punched, but seizing a stake from the fireplace, Hereward turned on his tormentors, laying about him with the stake. They tried to stab him with a pitchfork but he snatched a sword from one of the men, killed one and wounded several others and so made his escape. Once in the marshes again he found his horse and swiftly rode back to Ely by way of Sutton and Witchford.

But the King's orders were being quickly carried out. He commandeered all the available boats from Cottingham lake and surrounding areas so that more materials and men could be brought in over the flooded landscape. Great tree trunks were laid down and covered with sticks and stones to form a platform over the marsh on which the siege towers could be erected, and catapults for hurling stones were placed on the towers. The witch took her place on top of the leading tower and began her incantations so that she could lay a curse on the islanders. But Hereward and his men, disguised as labourers, had mingled with the workmen. They threw off their disguise, revealing their war-gear and weapons, and threw the enemy into confusion by setting fire to the reeds and willows of the fen and to the piles of unused wood around the siege towers, calling, in English, upon God to help them.

The whole structure and towers caught fire and the Normans fled in terror from the roaring flames and choking smoke. The very Fens themselves began to burn. The fire was whipped up by the wind and spread for half a kilometre into the swamp of reeds. That was how fire spread in the Fens. It also travelled out of sight below water level, in the peat. The Norman soldiers fled headlong into the swamp to get away from the fire, terrified by its raging, the noise of burning willows and the billowing smoke, which almost drove them mad with fear. Fire in peat is almost impossible to put out, it travels out of sight and erupts in explosions of steam as fire and water meet. Men crossing the affected area fell waist deep into burning peat. Hereward and his men, familiar with the dangers of the marsh, pursued the fleeing Normans, killing many trapped by the flames, and then retreated once more onto the Isle.

King William was enraged by his defeat and horror-stricken by his losses. His immediate revenge was to seize all the lands of the abbey of Ely that he could lay hands on and then distribute them to his men. News of this was carefully leaked to Abbot Thurstan and his monks, who began to have second thoughts about continuing to resist in case they lost everything. King William also let it be known through spies and secret agents that Earl Morcar and other nobles would be well-treated if they surrendered, but would suffer if they continued in their resistance. They well knew what could happen. Earl Edwin had decided not to stay with his brother at Ely and set out to make his way to Scotland. On the way, he was betrayed by three of his own men to a squad of Norman knights, caught in the open between a river and the sea, and slaughtered. His men took his head to King William, expecting a reward, but were themselves executed.

Abbot Thurstan contacted the King and offered to reveal to him how he could make his way onto the Isle from an unexpected direction. The King accepted the offer and Thurstan explained that he could make his way across the Cottingham lake (or Avering mere as it is alternatively referred to) by boat to a spot near the village of Little Thetford, a short distance from Ely town where the river was quite placid and could be easily crossed. William took the Abbot's advice.

It wasn't an easy journey. His army had to make a hard and winding march through the marshes to the mere, along a path revealed to the King by the monks. It was an area full of beds of flag iris covering and disguising treacherously marshy areas, a trap for the unwary. The path wound back and forth, so that men lost sight of one another in the eerie silence of the marsh. Sometimes they found themselves walking over the bodies of men and horses that had perished in the swamp. They had to travel through a marsh of horrid appearance and cross the many streams and watercourses running through the fens, wading through deep waters almost up to the level of their helmets and all the while harassed by attacks from the Fenlanders.

King William commandeered all available flat-bottomed fenland boats, the ancestors of the modern punt, to transport horses and catapults and the materials for yet another bridge. He had, of course, given up the idea of crossing near Aldreth because of the fires still raging in the marshes there.

Eventually he reached the area described by Abbot Thurstan, near Little Thetford, so brought up the boats carrying his catapults and set them up on the river bank. From there, he began to bombard the defenders, causing the unstable ground to shake and threatening everyone there with the risk of drowning. His 'engineers' now constructed a pontoon bridge built over a number of flat-bottomed boats lashed together and covered in willow branches, reeds and rushes. His bombardment softened up the opposition and he was able to lead his men across that weak and shaky pontoon bridge onto the Isle, driving back the remaining defenders with his horsemen.

From there, his forces swept forward in a pincer movement. One wing advanced directly towards Ely, along the old Roman road, Akeman Street (now the A10), while the other swept round through Witchford, where he accepted the surrender of Morcar and the nobles. Their

The Great Ouse at Little Thetford.　　　　　　　　*Copyright Peter Rex*

surrender did them no good, they had left it too late. Morcar, Siward Barn and Bishop Aethelwine were imprisoned. The bishop died shortly afterwards, Morcar remained a prisoner for life and Siward Barn was released when King William died so he fled abroad to Constantinople where he was said to have joined the Emperor's Varangian Guard. The other leaders of the Resistance were severely dealt with; some were blinded, others lost hands or feet. The ordinary rank and file were released unharmed.

While King William had been preparing his final attack, Hereward and his closest allies had left Ely on yet another raiding party from which he returned to find that Morcar and the others had surrendered and the King was already at Witchford. In his rage and despair he threatened to burn down the town but was persuaded by Ailwin, son of Sheriff Ordgar, that it was too late. He and his men then escaped through the Fens to take refuge in the Bruneswald, the great forest along the Fen edge in Northamptonshire and Huntingdonshire. There, for some months, he carried on with his attacks against the Norman King. Of his ultimate fate nothing very definite is known.

There are two conflicting versions. In one story, he was captured by King William, who sent the forces of seven shires to search the Bruneswald and capture him, only for Hereward to escape with the help of his gaoler, Robert of Harpole, who then persuaded King William to offer Hereward a pardon if he would enter his service. In that version, Hereward accepted, urged on by another noble lady, the widow of Earl Dolfin, called Aelftrude, and was given back some of his lands. (Hereward's first wife, Turfrida, had become a nun at Crowland and had recently died.) Hereward then lived out his life in retirement and, when he died, was also buried at Crowland. This version depends on two false clues. There was, according to Domesday Book, another Hereward who lived in Warwickshire, holding his lands in the service of the Bishop of Worcester and the Count of Mortain. Later story tellers have confused him with Hereward the Outlaw. Also, a later English rebel, Earl Waltheof of Northumbria, beheaded in 1075 for taking part in a revolt against King William, was buried at Crowland. So this is another case of mistaken identity.

The alternative version, written up in the 12th century by the poet Geoffrey Gaimar, says that, as in the first version, Hereward was reconciled to King William but went with him to the war in Maine where he made another fortune out of booty captured in the war. On his way home, he was ambushed by two dozen Norman knights seeking revenge against him, and died fighting single-handedly against overwhelming odds, killing about half of his assailants. Here, the poet is simply giving his hero a hero's death, in the literary convention of the time.

The most likely explanation is that, after seeing out the winter of 1071 in the Bruneswald, Hereward found England was becoming too dangerous for him so he and his men slipped away by sea to the Continent. Once there, he probably resumed his old career as a mercenary soldier and either died in battle or lived to return to England in the reign of William Rufus, where, living quietly in Norfolk, he died in old age. He might even at long last have been buried at Crowland. That he did survive in this way is suggested by evidence that at least two East Anglian families, at Terrington near Kings Lynn and Great Barton near Bury St. Edmunds, claimed descent from him. Wilburga of Terrington married a man called Hereward and claimed he was the grandson of "Hereward the Exile": a woman called 'Goda daughter of Hereward' became a nun and gave land at Great Barton, the property of her father Hereward and his father and grandfather, to the Abbey of Bury St. Edmunds.

That is the story of the real Hereward, whose exploits are recorded in the Anglo-Saxon Chronicle and in the Liber Eliensis. His exile and his lands, along with those of his father and grandfather, are mentioned in Domesday Book, 1086. His raid on Peterborough is related by Hugh Candidus in his History of Peterborough Abbey, written in the mid-12th Century, and in the Anglo-Saxon Chronicle for 1070-71, copied at Peterborough in about 1120. His other adventures are told in the Gesta Herewardi; the Book of the Exploits of Hereward, written partly by Leofric the deacon, who claimed to be Hereward's chaplain, and partly by the monk Richard of Ely, who wrote Book Two of the Liber Eliensis. Both the Gesta Herewardi (from Richard of Swaffham's Register from the early 13th century) and Richard of Ely's account in the Liber Eliensis are based on an account of Hereward's activities written before 1109 when the Abbacy became a Bishopric, and on the stories told by the monks of Ely and the Norman soldiers of the garrison.

Various popular stories about Hereward are attempts by later writers to claim him as the ancestor of the family of a minor Norman baron from Guernsey called Hugh Wake. Hugh married the daughter of a rich baron named Baldwin fitzGilbert, who had been given the Barony of Bourne in Lincolnshire by King Henry I. Among the lands attached to that barony were several of the farms once owned by Hereward or his father and, in order to build up his own reputation, Hugh's son, another Baldwin, claimed to be descended from Hereward himself. It was probably this Baldwin who began calling Hereward 'the Wake', in order to make people believe the claim. Hereward was called 'the Wake' because that family, the Wakes, claimed to be his descendants. They came from Guernsey, in the Channel Islands, and had always had the name of Wake; they did not get their name from Hereward. Baldwin fitzGilbert was a descendant of the Richard fitzGilbert who fought Hereward at the siege of Ely. Baldwin's wife was descended from a Breton called Enisan de Musard. Neither family has any connection whatsoever with the family of Hereward.

Hereward Asketilson stands for all those Englishmen who fought William the Conqueror and ensured that his conquest of England was bought at a heavy price in men and money, and took him more than five years to accomplish. The Norman Conquest did not begin and end with the Battle of Hastings.

Peter Rex was born then educated in Bristol, at St. Brendan's College then at the University where he graduated B.A. in History in 1952.

He entered teaching, and whilst working at a school in Spalding in 1959, became fascinated with the life and career of Hereward.

For more than twenty years he was Head of History and Political Studies at Princethorpe College, Warwickshire, and it was during this time that he gained his M.A. in Modern Historical and Political Studies from Coventry Polytechnic (now University). He was also for several years a member of the old London University Examinations Board A-level History Panel.

A few years after retirement he moved to Ely in 1997, and renewed his old interest in Hereward. His enthusiasm found him a publisher for two books resulting from his studies into Hereward and into resistance to the Norman Conquest.

Publications:

The English Resistance: the Underground War Against the Normans (Tempus 2004)
Hereward; the Last Englishman (Tempus 2005)
Harold II, the Doomed Saxon King (Tempus 2005)

In preparation, also for Tempus: *Edgar, King of the English*

Hugh Candidus Window, Peterborough Cathedral.
Copyright John Taylor

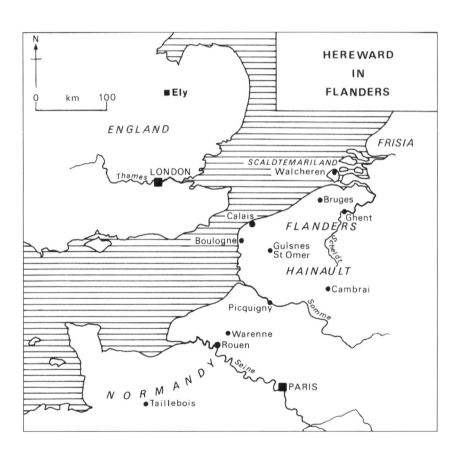

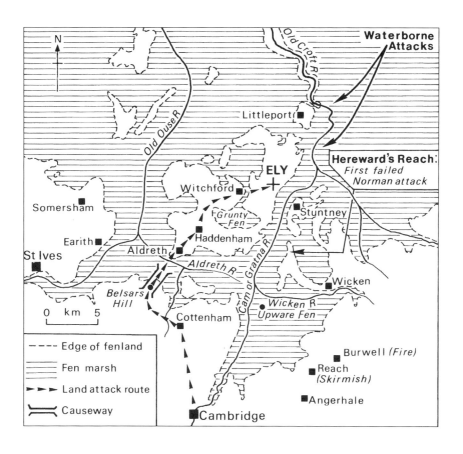